AF573898

Other books by Christopher Dewdney

Golders Green, The Coach House Press, 1972

A Palaeozoic Geology of London, Ontario, The Coach House Press, 1973

Fovea Centralis, The Coach House Press, 1975

Spring Trances in the Control Emerald Night, The Figures, 1978

Alter Sublime, The Coach House Press, 1980

Spring Trances in the Control Emerald Night & ***The Cenozoic Asylum***, The Figures, 1982

The Cenozoic Asylum, Délires, 1983

Predators of the Adoration: Selected Poems, McClelland and Stewart, 1983

The Immaculate Perception, House of Anansi Press, 1986

Permugenesis, Nightwood Editions, 1987

The Radiant Inventory, McClelland and Stewart, 1988

Recent Artifacts from the Institute of Applied Fiction, monograph from the Department of Rare Books, McGill University, 1990

Concordat Proviso Ascendant

Christopher Dewdney

A NATURAL HISTORY OF SOUTHWESTERN ONTARIO
BOOK III

THE FIGURES
1991

Cover painting: *Augusta, Late Afternoon* by John Moore, courtesy of Hirschl & Adler Modern.

The author wishes to thank the Toronto Arts Council, the Ontario Arts Council, and the Canada Council for their support.

Typeset in 14 point Baskerville by Eileen M. Clawson, Monterey, MA.

Distributed by *Small Press Distribution, Sun and Moon, Segue, Inland Book Company, Bookslinger,* and by Paul Green in the UK.

Publication of this book is supported by a grant from the National Endowment for the Arts, Literature Program, and by a gift from the Fund for Poetry.

The Figures, 5 Castle Hill, Great Barrington, MA 01230

Printed by Thomson-Shore, Inc., of Dexter, MI

ISBN 0-935724-42-7

Concordat Proviso Ascendant

David Heath, an English teacher at Xenia High School in Xenia, Ohio, was conducting an after-school drama class on an unusually hot June afternoon. Around 4:25 a student burst into the drama workshop, which was located in the school auditorium, and told them that a tornado was approaching.

"I came very close to telling everyone to forget it and to go through the dance number they were rehearsing again. Instead I jumped off the stage and told everyone to follow me so we could get a good view of the tornado. I imagined a funnel cloud in the sky that we could look at and then return to rehearsing. When we arrived at the front doors to the school we were astonished to see a viciously twisting column less than 200 yards away. Then, cars parked in front of the school began to bounce around. It was beyond belief. Someone said we'd better take cover so we all ran toward the center hall of the school. The lights went out just before we turned the corner and crouched against the walls on both sides of the corridor.

"Then the tornado struck. The weird thing was the sound of it, like the clattering of a thousand sets of Venetian blinds, along with tremendous crashing and grating sounds. When I opened my eyes a couple of times I saw large pieces of dirt and wood flying horizontally down the corridor. Then, for a moment, the wind stopped. One of the boys stood up, but I yelled at him to get down. Then the wind struck again with seemingly greater force. We were all hit with dirt, broken glass, mud, wood, heaven knows what else. I was still picking glass out of my scalp two days later. Finally it stopped, and there was total silence.

"When we stood up it was lighter than usual, and I looked up and noticed that the roof was entirely missing. Later we found out the ceiling of the auditorium had collapsed and that a school-bus lay upside down on the stage where we had been rehearsing."

Litany of Attributes

First let me name the miracles.
There is the miracle of your hair, obsidian mane
jet arborescence purple
by sunlight.
A sumerian flowerhead,
heavenly raiment of darkness.

There is the miracle of your wrists
breathlessly spare, amber & milk articulate
with blue veins. Impossible stems
for the miracle of your hands.

The authority of your hands, candid
unafraid of earth
of flesh, the necessities of love.
Pale pink pillowed palms
your slender, gracile fingers.

There is the miracle of your skin,
an ineluctable softness that extrapolates
your entire surface.

There is the miracle of your nipples
unearthly velvet. Honeyed spigots.

There is your brave nautical smile
afloat over your chin.

There is the miracle of your sex, heaven's gate
the interstice
of your thighs.
Night there.

And your legs
their long, almost ungainly grace.
The concord of your
lank, feral thighs.

Your feet
a celebration of earth &
all its miraculous parts,
triumph of muscle & tendon.
The slender sprawl of your toes
as you walk.

There is the miracle of you
in a moving taxi.
The languid authority of your carriage
an imperial choreography such
a convergent series of
graceful compensations.

Your back a facile treatise, vulnerable, curved.
Glissando of scapula & ribs. The
mitotic furrow of your spine.
There is the miracle of your hips,

charmed protrusions asserting
the frank endowment of your sex.
Your breasts smooth full temples outrageously
    adorned.

There is the miracle of your collarbones, avian &
delicate as your shoulders
their sharp dominion.

There is the miracle of your slightness,
your slender strength.
Our warrior of truth.

There is the miracle of your nose,
ineffable, angelic.

There is the miracle of your brow
clear & undaunted. Your neck
a heartbroken sanctuary.

There is the miracle of your eyes, their green pluck.
Feline & radiant.
The spirit I worship there.

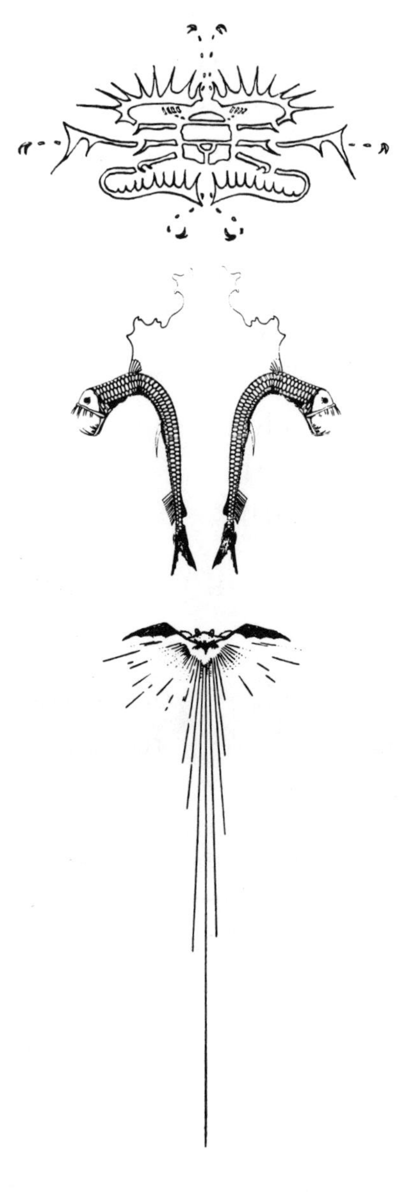

$$\left\{ O, C\text{n}, \begin{array}{c|c} g & l \\ k & l \\ \check{s} & \\ d & \\ \theta & \\ f & l \\ b & l \end{array} r,\ \begin{array}{c|} h \\ g \\ t \\ d \\ \theta \end{array} w,\ \begin{array}{c|} h \\ k \\ g \\ f \\ v \\ p \\ b \\ m \end{array} y(u),\ s \pm \begin{array}{c|c} k & w \\ t & r, \\ p & l \end{array} s \begin{array}{|c} k \\ t \\ l \\ n \\ f \\ p \\ m \\ w \end{array} + V + \left(\begin{array}{c} g \\ 3 \end{array}\right) O, \pm \begin{array}{c|} w \\ r \\ y\text{-}o \end{array}, C\text{-h}, \begin{array}{c|c} l & b,m,f \\ m & p \\ s & \\ s & k \\ l,n & g \\ s & t \\ & d \\ & s \end{array},\ \begin{array}{c|c} l & c \\ n & j \end{array},\ \begin{array}{rc|} & k \\ k & s \\ & n \\ & t \\ & d \\ & l \\ & n \\ & t \\ & p \\ & m\text{-pf} \end{array} \Theta, \pm \begin{array}{c} t/d \\ s/z \\ st/zd \end{array} \right\} \begin{array}{l} C, C, > C, \\ \\ \text{(OVERRIDING RESTRICTION)} \end{array}$$

SHE IS BEYOND YOU NOW. Her piscine features embryonic & dissipated with wisdom. Her nakedness possessed each time a seething harlequin of erectile sequins. Her lips aching with honey. The sky darkening with dreams.

There is a language to predicate the adoration.

And the water, its essence an alarming grace unfolding past the edge of your control. Breeding miraculous witness. Command spillover. Trembling mica electron thunder. Distant blue spruce shimmer vaguely translucent pagodas rising like glass temples in the dusk. The ammonoid's nacreous lustre, iridescent stage lights in a cretaceous theatre. Slow-motion August trees, the Huron clay bluffs blue in the lake haze & at night the stars rain glittering onto the beach. Pyritized mother of pearl a refraction so ancient the dreams are blackened. This most devonian of raptures. A vowel away from the discrete crystals wherein her rude beauty gives way to angels. Soil the cumulative evidence of life processes, a recursive matrix & husky skin of utility stretched over the original rock. Limestone the accumulation of this evidence. As the planet turns into the photon irradiation of dawn. Our debt to the truth.

Beneath the lake a room. The water is electric. The smallest perturbation being transmitted through the whole undiminished. For its membrane is the precursor of the cellular envelope, budding cauldrons at the base of the falls. It is living. It whispers & moans & there are a thousand voices in the rapids. It is the medium of choice for internal predators.

Daylilies waxen cups of orange & red conspiring in the late afternoon sun.

Dazzling cellular lattice. Rattlesnake point.

Dusty milkweeds at the side of the road. Summer cricket fields phasing a pointillistic audio plane. Waves of wind in the leaves transparent molasses. Insect voyeurs.

It is night and there is a yearning in the wind. Your heart a dusky corporeal fragrance streaming into the stars. And in the moonlight you can see the underwater trees. Devonian ocean floor commands the summer sky a fossil sea. Spicebush, oak & sassafras. The mouth of the Ausable. Blue evening dunes of the Pinery. The morning sun a coral resonance in the crowns of the trees. Leafless spring forest glowing tide against the sun fissured escarpment. Incremental heat of the vernal arc high over Collingwood.

Specific mist of August pink & gold. A morning light all day. The forest shade almost colloidal, darkening under the looming thunderheads. Lilacs. Nicotinia. A penetrating dampness, limp clothes & paper, the subway floors sweating under her sandals. Gracile her slim body. Gamelan the thrill of her hands. A proton decay cavern under the south shore of Erie. Her toes an almost Fibonacci sequence, her lips tasting of unknown cities. Rain shimmering in the Zildjian forest. A bat flying through Allen Gardens. Glass membrane ruptured into the June night sky, itself an infernal mosaic of irregular cobalt tiles, prismatic sparks at their interstices. Her sex flushed in the fire lithe under the trees. Words unable me to speak to you. There is a path for you hear if you see it. She was paradise renewed a tangible & immaculate dream. Blue the colour of opium in a dream once. As expensive as the sun reflected on blonde hair through tinted hotel glass.

AWKWARD MAMMALIAN BLOSSOMS in cool sunlight the memory of childhood not ours. Occidental blue of April afternoons the distant north an aerial clarion in the heavens. Tough green sexual resilience of buds in the cold air, beryl spires insinuate the heaving soil. As if the sky would quicken and reveal another scale of perspective, a giant immanence of dreams born in wordless childhood musings. The April plainness of building materials on cold grey afternoons. Provisional shelter. And at night the glistening celestial machinery. The sky deepening with stars, crescent of the new moon just setting above the glow of the sunset. Concrete technical reality. There is a heraldry in creation unseen. Stoney morning brook, sparkling water beads the optical distillation of the previous night's stars. Star dew. The rain we pray for. Recognition in the May foliage, secret arboreal house of dreams & wind. Star corridors. The axis insatiable. Labialithe.

A temporal music where each successive note is justified only by its predecessor. A harmony such that the edge of dissonance suspends the speed of beauty. Grey and gold escarpment the October rain. Let them all see it, May nights a reality of precise darkness gushing the wildest hot metals as you spurt dimly into her red shift depths. Bronze rivers sinuous with age. Boreal rawness of the early June foliage. Huron palisade the plateau forest of the escarpment.

A single firefly, portentous intermittent star wending silently through the dim canyons of spruce. Meandering green ember in the solid obsidian glass night. A supernumerary planet adding its strange light to the stars. Unearthly machinery of the forest darkness. Nightshade. Low frequency rumble of the planetary surface. The night before the day after. Summer sun a cool furnace in the furthest depths of the moon. The avenues we drive home on. Solstice moon waxing pale in the afternoon sky. Evergreen. Chlorophyll & haemoglobin. Red Haven. The music frightening & joyous. I have the vehicle to take you there, its gleaming fuselage a landscape foreshortened by velocity.

Take command of the senses. You are all that you see. Cardinal in the redbud. The lake milky blue green under the purple sky of an approaching electrical storm. Something ironic in you which is not fully formed. This moment gone too far. Delirium in the summer wind. The midnight cicada. Proliferation of crickets. The horizon a window of impossible perspective, multi-layered stratus & cumulonimbus. Decalcomania of deciduous clouds. A path is the least resistance.

Cap & talus of the escarpment diminishing into perspective haze at our sides. Grimsby ravine an irresistible river of gravity, sensual cushion over the unwavering creek. Her abdomen pale cream curdled with muscles. Her power a private delight arched & supple. Her thrall of nakedness. Pseudoscorpions under shoes on the landing. Fruitflies. Peaches. The October moon a glaucous eye through alto-stratus. A life refined to one unbearable moment. Love a semantics you invent between. Her touch a thrilling cellular wind blowing through my nervous system. This glistening skin & sweet absence. The mild labile hysteria of gulls.

Lustful engine of summer metal quickening in the late March railway soil. Hot metal shaft of the vernal axis naked under bare sumac branches. Her breath an exquisite musk reminiscent of the osmoderma. The Elora Gorge, summer reptile sunbanks the cool morning cedar forest aloft on each side. Ocular water sliding lager beneath quick ledges. Limestone caves. There is an ineffable music which lingers in the charged air over the rapids. A single note triggers intangible symphonies, their strange harmonies blend into the fabric of all sound.

Late night rhapsody of the ecliptic,

ultramarine spangled with planets. The looming almost frightening wisdom of children. The still city a planar crystal lattice dreaming under the bright shoals of Lake Iroquois. Our orgasm an embodied mutual description. A forest trail is a dance, a re-enactment. It is an encoded history, the cumulative response of prior travellers to a given topography. A path is a mnemonic calisthenics, a sequence of implicit responses which every traveller not only recounts but alters slightly with their passing. The river mist pungent malt of liquid leaves. Branches, roots, boulders & niches, the landscape proffers itself for our progress on the slopes. Seminal blue electric glow of the waterfall. Demerara floor of the cedar forest striped with sun. Limestone terraces marking the descent of the ancestral river. Ramparts encased in the cedarn canopy, itself a photon greenhouse evanescent in the July heat. Each bank of the gorge an interior unknowable to the other.

Darkness comes early in the gorge, twisting along the paths like a warm river wind, a corporeal zephyr. Chronology skewed with silence in the chiming afternoon. An autumn indistinguishable from morning proceeding like no other. The gorge sweating in the white heat of the rapids. Cedar, hemlock, white pine & birch. Elm & ash beyond. Gorge patrol. Dry riverbed of twilight & night in the cedar forest, fragrant darkness spilling down the shallow fossil valley.

Toronto interglacial overcast, a temperate deciduous freshwater marine light. Metal at high speed. White clay bluffs & summer interiors burgundy & pale dusty green. Purple stone. Wood smoke an evening mist the water pellucid jelly. Moiré of ripples an inverse solution to the equation of the shoreline. The wind in the canopy a sudden aerial rapids. This nightriver, gentle grade & bowl & groove.

Faintly pungent, acrid limestone river rank from trickle falls luxurious with moss. Still grace the rainforest mist intermittent showers retained by the canopy released. Mercurial chipmunks, warm tubular & insistent, their lingering stripes. Blue ash. The forest roots a semiology we can just barely comprehend. I have the music to take you there, its gleaming fuselage just beyond the curve of this hill. Drone of the cicadas adorning the beech temple, serpentine roots bursting the foundation stones. Underwater shelves of limestone. Salamanders moist beneath dry forest rocks. Dolomite glistening with crystals, calcite chambers within. Bracken. Quantum flight of the hoverfly. Still heavy air, thunder low in the distance. The elastic twang of a bullfrog locates the shallows. The night gorge pointillistic with fireflies, moonlight on waves. Trembling mica electron thunder an underground city.

SHE IS LIQUID DARKNESS occult with desire. An abandoned airplane hangar, scattered curls of corrugated steel littering the floor punctate with sun discs. The naked air electric anticipation we unite glistening in the radiance of giant atmospheric machines rising above the horizon. The sky filled with sound furious insistent joy as she cries, aching chorus of electroluminescent orgasm. Heat-bleached August fields. Sun-burned foliage in the shallow ravine. Cool green lawns under moist tree caverns. Earthen paths packed & powdered. Lambton forest a cool sensual intuition. Limestone trestles under the railway bridge. Night perfume of the magnolia blossoms. Cicadas shimmering in the late summer trees. Storm flooded city streets. Aromatic twigs. Her incendiary hands. September heatwave, a single katydid rasping in the night tree. Humid wind & magnified leaf shadows a restless cinema under the backyard floodlight. Wild grapes purple on the vine. Particulate smoky blue haze of hot October afternoons. Indian summer in the Berkshires. Manhattan. Wild rhododendrons in the Hudson valley.

By becoming myself I have become someone else. My adoration the natural fulfillment of her sacral narcissism. She is eros displayed. Lank salient grace of her thighs as she consumes me. There is a forest with ferns primaeval down there. She drew a shade of stratus. Chunks of stone erode into Mayan friezes. Gold scarabs at Clark point. She won't stop until you've come unnaturally again and again. Creek newts frankly relaxed in the sandy aquarium delta foliage. An otter near the forks of the Ervin and Grand. Cedar roots dowsing Silurian strata. Prodigious acrobatics of the mud swallows.

She is here now. Her face a dark lantern blossoming in the twilight. Every path the most expedient solution of opposite destinations. She lies down amongst the ferns. Manitoulin cecropias. A flute lost in the sound of the rapids. Scarab grubs harboured in the scrub oaks. We merge in the windy forest, in the rushing neo-silence of a hot August wind, in the mute aqueous clamour of leaves under the wild hush of the canopy. Our clothes sullen layers of skin. Our giant bodies a glistening electric surface continuous with the forest. Close upon us now this afternoon an atmosphere of flesh. The smell of rain in the wind. August enthralled in the cool depths of the lake. Mudpuppy. Hellbender. September heatwave stone temple haze along the beach distant signal fires glimmering orange. Her water broke the slow fall of evening leaves, waves of silver green the boughs above human creatures coupling wondrous beneath. Chlorophyll mist. The sky ringing with our music.

ALIVE WITH SELF REPRESENTATION the forest is a temple of compliance amongst the protective emblems of the natural kingdom. Our path a dark sweetness, musky tribute to your surrender. Your face miraculous stone sweating in the August heat. The somnambulistic lucidity of dusk's intent. The sky a dream of cirrus & aquamarine, deep purple silhouettes of distant airplanes descending into the edge of night. High evening a secret joyous darkness internally illuminated by a fossil sun. Night windows of a large home near the river, porch light & screen door. In the cool darkness of the basement nocturnal children interlock within the necessities of desire. Their faces animal flowers insensate with beauty. Tropical leaf theatre under the stadium lights. The stars through hot leaves our bodies dusted with forest & surely engaged by a slender path. Indistinguishable in the twilight we rub ourselves with dirt & slide mucous pink into each other again and again, the merging earth our union & we ache for the river music, a blanket of silence. Its impassive interior a mute piscine concourse. Our continuous night eyes. We are intruders in our own house the incandescent lights a peripheral flicker our bodies smudged with soil. Our reflection in the picture window the night trees behind. You come rubbing against me we come androgynous we come first as two boys & then as two women. A cistern of water in the bathtub, in the sink. A rainbarrel in the garden & in the stream our bodies indissoluble within the warm river currents there. Gradual accumulation of insects at the porch light, a glittering raiment. Our bodies quick & light in the night air. Dusty pink evening at the botanical gardens. Neural storms in her pupils. A magnetic field suddenly explicit around each tree as a flock of birds erupts from one & is sucked into another. Avian prominence the lines of force. There are salamanders nearby.

GOTHIC GEOMETRY OF THE LYCOPOD forest. The axis of symmetry explicit in the angular lattice of the canopy. Rustling flight of a giant dragonfly. Its cellophane wings glinting in the Carboniferous sunlight, a vanishing airy chain of after-images. The humidity of the gorge forest is higher than the surrounding area. A world millions of years in the past. Snake doctor, helicopter, red doppler shift. My camp a rainforest vigil here at the transition zone. The camouflaged wings of the moth are pure representation, the mean portion of a forage specific ambience. A path is an intra-species engineering project, a passive collaboration. Distant rumble of thunder older even than the shark. With every instinctive fibre of your being. Iridescent blue scarab deep within the petals of the rose.

Watersnakes basking on the sunny river banks. Ion shadow of the thunderhead hovering sightless over the forest a charmed garden. Fabric of reality parting slightly just before the lightning. Swimming naked in the warm night river. Umbilical tornado. Copper oxide & limestone chambers. On a field sable a lynx rampant. The crown of night. The margin of heaven and earth blurred this evening. Moonrise.

The water is continuous music enacting the bias of the valley. In the distance are ranch-style bungalows constructed in the mid-1950s. Adolescents shimmer in the corruption of self-consciousness, their limbs bronze & gold in the summer sun. The wings of the polyphemous moth are a dialogue between two alien critical conventions, an operational diptych, the doors of the sacred. The sunlight pale stained glass green, the forest a cathedral, its floor studded with the remains of ancient temples dedicated to unknown gods. Elora gorge an erogenous wound in the surface of the limestone. Dusky salamanders' translucent licorice speckled with silver. There is a landscape which corresponds to each station of the heart, a geography for every phase of our lives.

The Elora gorge is a rift valley in time, an amphitheatre of cedar & limestone. The hot green twilight of the forest depths. Decaying Hindu temples, each built on the crumbling summit of its predecessor. Roots & vines form twisted lattices over the limestone walls. Umbrella magnolias & blue ash. Giant swallowtail butterfly momentary cadmium in the shadowy interior of the forest. Water wrestling with rocks in the depths of the rapids. The air in the gorge still & heavy, the sky misting over into a featureless bright grey haze, maximum heat of early evening. Distant thunder. Nighthawks, crickets, bats & raccoons, unbroken wild continuum into the centers of the great lake cities.

CUESTA & VALE TOPOGRAPHY. Bright hypnotic splendour of the solstice noon. A dragonfly lands on her shoulder, its rainbow wings glittering in the June sunlight. Endless summer night of the high arctic Eocene. Her ancestral devonian arms sinister. Just past the pre-melanization peak of the swallowtails in the heart of the Pleistocene concourse. Giant catalpa trees bearing signal standards of white blossoms, profound and lucid in the cloudless solar morning. On still nights their fragrance a redolent penumbra, a nocturnal skirt of perfume. Limestone trestles of the railway bridge erotic monuments in the television foliage of an industrial age summer. Barberry blossoms' spermy pungence on hot June nights. Cartilaginous sex. Grey diffuse light of memory, a sensualizing texture irrupting & sweetening everything with cosmic nostalgia for the moment. Each second a prodigal return, reality re-corporealized with recognition.

Fess engrailed. Mammatocumulus illuminated from underneath by the setting sun. Night hardwood on the summer campus, corinthian columns ascending through successive tiers of concentric leaf mobiles, deciduous candelabra. Their outlines slowly rippling in the hallucinogenic mist of the nocturnal forest. Indiscernable from the veritable animation of the night wind. Delicate wallpaper clouds near the full moon in the cinema blue night. The forest a room we dissipate into, particularize. Involute masters of uncertain dimensions.

Muscular black night wind. Dry summer night wind dusty with stars. The faint brown band of skin around the middle of my cock. Blowing clear & hot from the boreal summer.

Jerusalem wind through northern valleys the stirring of dark mountains in the alchemical night, giant sensual gods sculpted in basalt. Desert wind a thousand years old and clear as deuterium pools, a wind empty through our hearts, their mysterious longing. A wind which pulls us wordless from our bodies, the rushing final wind. The historical wind erotic & spiritual, stone dieties coupling on the walls of jungle temples. Eocene nacht-music.

So fair our green. Testicular sacs of the oriole nest, winged persimmons in her green vigilance. The honeysuckle's buzzing aura of insects. Hummingbirds a demonstration of convergent evolution, aves radiating into an insect niche, tailfeathers disappearing in functional mimicry of the sphinx moth. Sun sporadically from behind hazy cumulus clouds, the lake impenetrable with mist. Stiff, incremental surge of the growing trees. The forest is the perpetual, internal twilight of dream. I am the fisher king of my unconscious. Up-grading tree climbing theory. Root cascades on rocks, gnarled retainers for terraced humus waterfalls, re-enactment of a fossil rapids. Delightfully uneven terrain. Forest rocks luminous with condensation, green antler velvet congealed into stone. The clamour of the storm lags in noisy streams.

DISTANT APARTMENT COMPLEXES MOODY empires of light, subdued orange constellations in the hazy twilight. The revelation of the rainy day. Late night resurrection of a forgotten love, a vanished civilization, where the waning moon is the accusational eye of a discarded lover. Velvet metaphysics in the dusty light on the trunks of the norway spruce, cicada husks at their bases. Windbreak colonnade. Love's absence is still love, the heart a celestial wound. August a certain Aegean light through us all. The beach a commotion of light and waves, cries of gulls and children blending in the wind. Honeysuckle vines redolent with evening, a dusky corona of ruby throats. Surprising articulation of children's backs, an advanced hominid wisdom. Wild cherry gum on raw copper. The dull gleam of tin roofs. Field of hydroelectric power flickering in the continuous darkness at the bottom of the lake.

She is delightfully augmented. In the distance vandals break windows in a deserted factory, disembodied locus of fear. Meander. She walks almost laboriously around her endowments, a libidinous & circuitous grace. She is crippled with sex, ripe fruit on a slender bough. Resume the broken discourse of the gods. A quick vertigo of lust. The milky way wheeling on a hub of antimatter through abandoned zodiacs in the mysterious depths of an intergalactic summer night. A continuous indoor atmosphere which extends uniformly & infinitely in all directions.

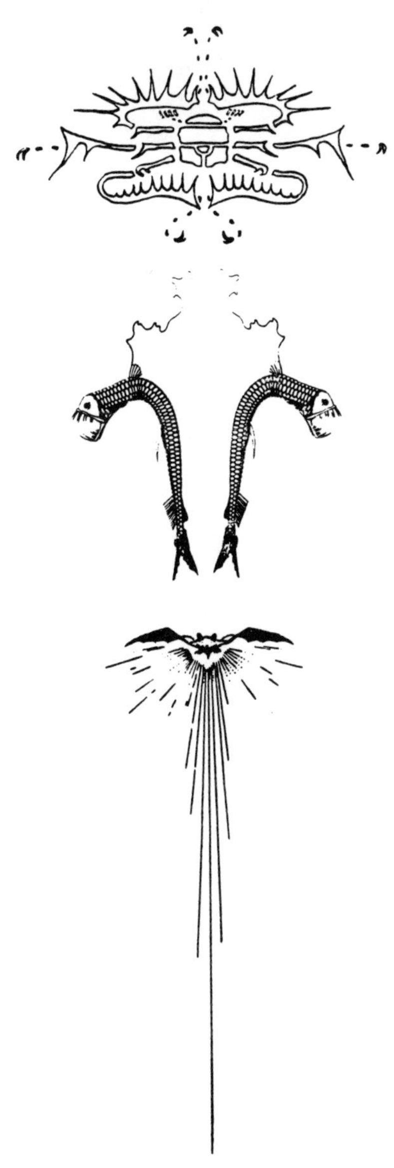

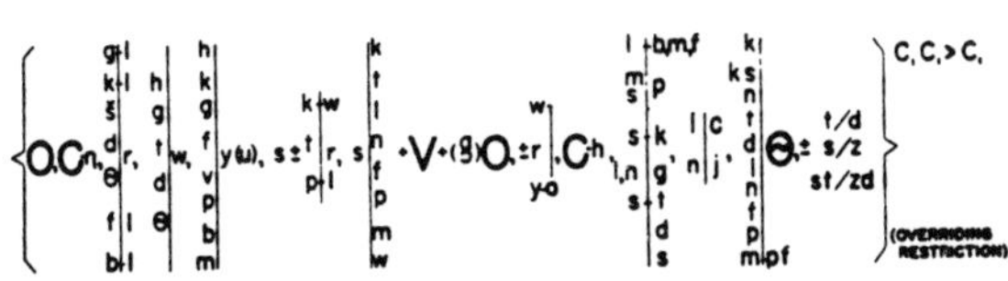

C, C, > C,
t/d
s/z
st/zd
(OVERRIDING RESTRICTION)

A NOTE ON THE TEXT:

Concordat Proviso Ascendant is part of a longer work called *A Natural History of Southwestern Ontario*, which is a compendium of particulars written from the inside of its subject. These particulars inventory a personal, regional identity directly informed by natural history. Many of the creatures, locales and weather conditions in this poem have their correlates around the globe, particularly in tropical regions.

Because *A Natural History of Southwestern Ontario* is a ritual text each book has to be preceded by the firsthand account of someone who has been *inside* a tornado. This is a primal, sacred experience of nature's most extreme and random violence. However, it is a cruelty without malice derived from an impartiality at the heart of nature, and the universe, for that matter. Ultimately our cosmos functions as an inhuman, yet intimate, phenomenology to which we impute deistic attributes because we cannot conceive of anything so subtle and complex operating without consciousness as we know it.

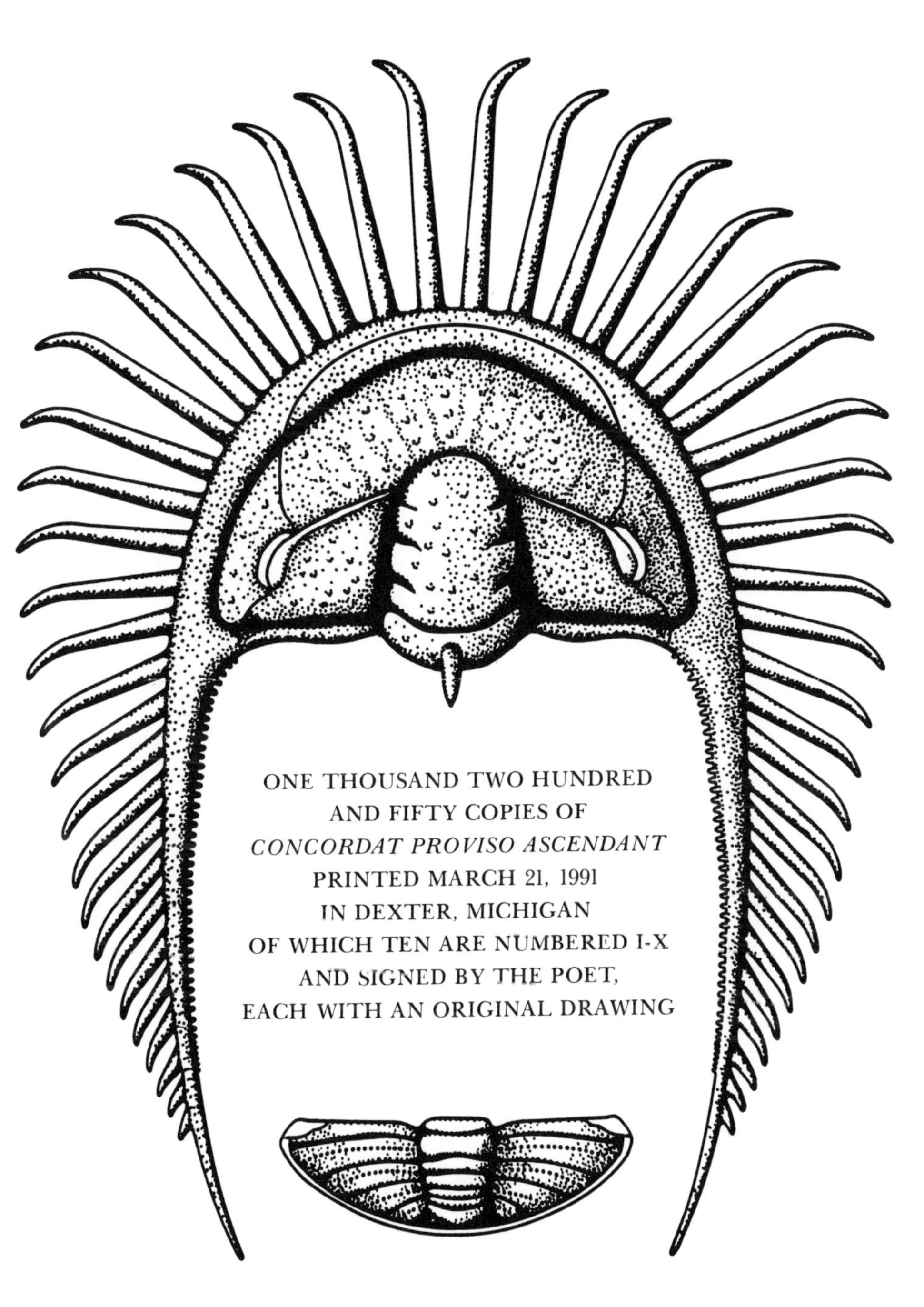

ONE THOUSAND TWO HUNDRED
AND FIFTY COPIES OF
CONCORDAT PROVISO ASCENDANT
PRINTED MARCH 21, 1991
IN DEXTER, MICHIGAN
OF WHICH TEN ARE NUMBERED I-X
AND SIGNED BY THE POET,
EACH WITH AN ORIGINAL DRAWING

Photo by Paul Orenstein

CHRISTOPHER DEWDNEY was born in London, Ontario, in 1951. The author of ten books of poetry, he teaches creative writing and postmodern literature at York University in Toronto and has lectured and read widely across Canada, the United States and Great Britain.

THE FIGURES

Rae Armantrout *Extremities* $4.00
Paul Auster *Wall Writing* o. p.
David Benedetti *Nictitating Membrane* $5.00
Steve Benson *As Is* $5.00
Steve Benson *Blue Book* $12.50
Alan Bernheimer *Cafe Isotope* $5.00
John Brandi *Diary from a Journey to the Middle of the World* $6.00
Summer Brenner *From the Heart to the Center* $5.00
Summer Brenner *The Soft Room* $6.00
David Bromige *My Poetry* $8.00
Laura Chester *My Pleasure* $5.00
Laura Chester *Watermark* $6.00
Tom Clark *Baseball* $6.50
Clark Coolidge *At Egypt* $7.50
Clark Coolidge *The Crystal Text* $10.00
Clark Coolidge *Melencolia* $3.50
Clark Coolidge *Mine: The One That Enters the Stories* $7.50
William Corbett *Remembrances* $4.00
Michael Davidson *Analogy of the Ion* $4.00
Michael Davidson *The Prose of Fact* o. p.
Lydia Davis *Story and Other Stories* $7.50
Christopher Dewdney *Concordat Proviso Ascendant* $7.50
Christopher Dewdney *Spring Trances in the Control Emerald Night & The Cenozoic Asylum* $8.00
Johanna Drucker *Italy* $5.00
Barbara Einzig *Disappearing Work* o. p.
Elaine Equi *Accessories* $4.00
Norman Fischer *On Whether or Not to Believe In Your Mind* $7.50
Kathleen Fraser *Each Next* $7.50
Gloria Frym *Back to Forth* $7.50
Merrill Gilfillan *River Through Rivertown* $6.00
Michael Gizzi *Just Like A Real Italian Kid* $4.00
John Godfrey *Midnight on Your Left* $6.00
Lyn Hejinian *Writing is an Aid to Memory* $7.50
Paul Hoover *Idea* $7.50
Fanny Howe *Introduction to the World* $5.00
Ron Padgett *The Big Something* $7.50
Ron Padgett & Clark Coolidge *Supernatural Overtones* $7.50
Bob Perelman *a.k.a.* $8.00
Bob Perelman *Captive Audience* $6.00
Bob Perelman *The First World* $5.00
Bob Perelman *7 Works* o. p.
Tom Raworth *Tottering State* $11.50

Tom Raworth *Writing* $10.00
Stan Rice *Some Lamb* o. p.
Kit Robinson *Down and Back* $5.00
Kit Robinson *Covers* $4.00
Stephen Rodefer *The Bell Clerk's Tears Keep Flowing* $12.00 (Cloth)
Stephen Rodefer *Emergency Measures* $7.50
Stephen Rodefer *Four Lectures* $7.50
Peter Schjeldahl *The 7 DAYS Art Columns* $12.50
James Schuyler *Early in '71* o. p.
Ron Silliman *Tjanting* $10.00
Ron Silliman *What* $10.00
Julia Vose *Moved Out on the Inside* $6.00
Guy Williams *Selected Works 1876-1982* With an Essay
by Gus Blaisdell $10.00
Geoffrey Young *Rocks and Deals* $4.00
Geoffrey Young *Subject to Fits* $8.00